# COUNTRY

**Formal Name:** Federal Republic of Nigeria.

**Short Form:** Nigeria.

**Term for Citizen(s):** Nigerian(s).

**Capital:** Abuja has been the capital of Nigeria since December 12, 1991. Previously, the capital was Lagos.

**Major Cities:** According to preliminary results of the 2006 census and subsequent estimates, the most populous cities in Nigeria are Lagos (about 8 million), Kano (3.8 million), Ibadan (2.6 million), Kaduna (1.7 million), Port Harcourt (1.3 million), and Benin City (1.1 million).

**Independence:** Nigeria achieved independence from the United Kingdom on October 1, 1960.

**Public Holidays:** A national holiday commemorating independence is celebrated on October 1. Other holidays are New Year's (January 1), Eid al Kabir (Feast of the Sacrifice—movable date based on the Islamic calendar), Eid al Maulud (Birth of the Prophet—movable date based on the Islamic calendar), Easter (movable date in March or April), Workers' Day (May 1), Eid al Fitr (End of Ramadan—movable date based on the Islamic calendar), Christmas (December 25), and Boxing Day (December 26).

**Flag:** Nigeria's flag consists of three equal vertical bands of green, white, and green.

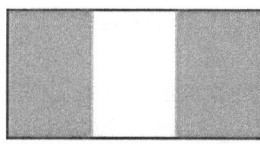

**Click to Enlarge Image**

# HISTORICAL BACKGROUND

Several dominant themes in Nigerian history are essential for understanding contemporary Nigerian politics and society. First, the spread of Islam, predominantly in the north but later in southwestern Nigeria as well, began a millennium ago. The creation of the Sokoto Caliphate in the jihad (holy war) of 1804–8 brought most of the northern region and adjacent parts of Niger and Cameroon under a single Islamic government. The great extension of Islam within the area of present-day Nigeria dates from the nineteenth century and the consolidation of the caliphate. This history helps account for the dichotomy between north and south and the divisions within the north that have been so pronounced during the colonial and postcolonial eras. Second, the slave trade across both the Sahara Desert and the Atlantic Ocean had a profound influence on virtually all parts of Nigeria. The transatlantic trade in particular accounted for the forced migration of perhaps 3.5 million people between the 1650s and the 1860s, while a steady stream of slaves flowed north across the Sahara for a millennium, ending only at the beginning of the twentieth century. Within Nigeria, slavery was widespread and bore social implications that are still evident. Conversion to Islam and the spread of Christianity were intricately associated with issues relating to slavery and with efforts to promote political and cultural autonomy. Third, the colonial era was relatively brief, lasting only six decades or so depending on the part of Nigeria, but it unleashed such rapid change that the full impact is still felt in the contemporary period.

**Early History:** All evidence suggests the early settlement of Nigeria millennia before the spread of agriculture 3,000 years ago. The earliest culture in Nigeria is identifiable by the distinctive artifacts of the Nok people. These skilled artisans and ironworkers flourished between the fourth century B.C. and the second century A.D. in a large area above the confluence of the Niger and Benue rivers. The Nok achieved a level of material development not repeated in the region for nearly 1,000 years.

Long before 1500, much of present-day Nigeria was divided into states, which can still be linked to the modern ethnic groups that trace their history to the origins of these states. These early states included the Yoruba kingdoms, the Edo kingdom of Benin, the Hausa cities, and Nupe. In addition, numerous small states to the west and south of Lake Chad were absorbed or displaced in the course of the expansion of Kanem, centered to the northeast of Lake Chad. Borno, initially the western province of Kanem, became independent in the late fourteenth century.

The sixteenth century marked a high point in the political history of northern Nigeria. During this period, the Songhai Empire reached its greatest limits, stretching from the Senegal and Gambia rivers in the far west and incorporating part of Hausaland in the east. At the same time, the Sayfawa Dynasty of Borno asserted itself, conquering Kanem and extending its control westward to Hausa cities that were not under Songhai imperial rule. For almost a century, much of northern Nigeria was part of one or the other of these empires, and after the 1590s, Borno dominated the region for 200 years. Despite Borno's hegemony, the Hausa states wrestled for ascendancy among themselves for much of the seventeenth and eighteenth centuries.

**European Slave Trade in West Africa:** By 1471 Portuguese ships had reconnoitered the West African coast south as far as the Niger Delta. Portugal's lasting legacy for Nigeria was its initiation of the transatlantic slave trade. The Portuguese monopoly on West African trade was broken at the end of the sixteenth century when Portugal's influence was challenged by the rising naval power of the Netherlands. The Dutch took over Portuguese trading stations on the coast that were the source of slaves for the Americas. French and British competition later undermined the Dutch position, and Britain became the dominant slaving power in the eighteenth century.

By the end of the eighteenth century, the area that was to become Nigeria was far from a unified country. Furthermore, the orientation of north and south was entirely different. The savanna states of Hausaland and Borno in the north had experienced a difficult century of political insecurity and ecological disaster but otherwise continued in a centuries-long tradition of slow political and economic change that was similar to other parts of the savanna. The southern areas near the coast, by contrast, had been swept up in the transatlantic slave trade. Political and economic change had been rapid and dramatic. By 1800 Oyo, a constitutional monarchy, governed much of southwestern Nigeria, while the Aro, another polity, had consolidated southeastern Nigeria into a confederation. Both Oyo and the Aro confederacy were major trading partners of the slave traders from Europe and North America.

In the first decade of the nineteenth century, two unrelated developments that were to have a major influence on virtually all of the area that is now Nigeria ushered in a period of radical change. First, between 1804 and 1808 the Islamic holy war of Usman dan Fodio established the Sokoto Caliphate, a loose confederation of emirates centered in northwestern Nigeria. By the middle of the nineteenth century, when the Sokoto Caliphate was at its greatest extent, it comprised 30 emirates and the capital district of Sokoto. All the important Hausa emirates, including Kano, the wealthiest and most populous, were directly under Sokoto. Second, in 1807 Britain declared the transatlantic slave trade to be illegal, an action that occurred at a time when Britain itself was responsible for shipping more slaves to the Americas than any other country. Although the transatlantic slave trade did not end until the 1860s, other commodities, especially palm oil, gradually replaced it. The shift in trade had serious economic and political consequences in the interior, which led to increasing British intervention in the affairs of Yorubaland and the Niger Delta.

**Colonial Nigeria:** In 1885 at the Berlin Conference, the European powers attempted to resolve their conflicts of interest in Africa by allotting areas of exploitation. The conferees also enunciated the principle, known as the "dual mandate," that the interests of both Europe and Africa would best be served by maintaining free access to the African continent for trade and by providing Africa with the benefits of Europe's civilizing mission. Britain's claims to a sphere of influence in the Niger Basin were acknowledged formally, but it was stipulated that only effective occupation would secure full international recognition. In the end, pressure from France and Germany hastened the establishment of effective British occupation and the creation of protectorates in northern and southern Nigeria.

Frederick Lugard, who assumed the position of high commissioner of the Protectorate of Northern Nigeria in 1900, was occupied with transforming the commercial sphere of influence inherited from the Royal Niger Company into a viable territorial unit under effective British political control. His objective was to conquer the entire region and to obtain recognition of the British protectorate by its indigenous rulers, especially the Fulani emirs of the Sokoto Caliphate. Lugard's campaign systematically subdued local resistance, using armed force when diplomatic measures failed. Lugard's success in northern Nigeria has been attributed to his policy of indirect rule, which called for governing the protectorate through the rulers who had been defeated. If the emirs accepted British authority, abandoned the slave trade, and cooperated with British officials in modernizing their administrations, the colonial power was willing to confirm them in office. Lugard's immediate successor, Hugh Clifford (1919–25), introduced a diametrically opposed approach emphasizing Western values. In contrast to Lugard, Clifford restricted the power of the northern emirs by scaling back indirect rule, while in the south he saw the possibility of building an elite educated in European-style schools.

British colonialism created Nigeria, joining diverse peoples and regions in an artificial political entity with little sense of a common Nigerian nationality. Inconsistencies in British policy reinforced cleavages based on regional animosities by attempting simultaneously to preserve the indigenous cultures of each area and to introduce modern technology and Western political and social concepts. In the north, appeals to Islamic legitimacy upheld the rule of the emirs, so that nationalist sentiments there were decidedly anti-Western. Modern nationalists in the south, whose thinking was shaped by European ideas, opposed indirect rule, which had entrenched what was considered to be an anachronistic ruling class in power and shut out the Westernized Nigerian elite.

**Independence and Civil War:** By an act of the British Parliament, Nigeria became an independent country within the Commonwealth on October 1, 1960. In 1963 Nigeria became a republic within the Commonwealth. The change in status called for no practical alteration of the constitutional system. The president, elected to a five-year term by a joint session of the parliament, replaced the crown as the symbol of national sovereignty and the British monarch as head of state. Nnamdi Azikiwe became the republic's first president.

Although the first postindependence parliamentary elections were held in December 1964, the nation's leadership in the several decades following independence was determined by coup, not by election, and by military, rather than civilian, government. One of the most important developments during the 1960s was the declaration of independence by the Eastern Region in 1967, followed by a 30-month civil war. In the face of increased sectarian violence, the Eastern Region's military governor, Lieutenant Colonel Chukwuemeka Odumegwu Ojukwu, was under pressure from Igbo (also seen as Ibo) officers to assert greater independence from the Federal Military Government (FMG). Ultimately, on May 30, 1967, Ojukwu proclaimed the independent Republic of Biafra, named after the Bight of Biafra. He cited as the principal cause for this action the government's inability to protect the lives of predominantly Igbo easterners and suggested its culpability in genocide.

Initially, the FMG launched "police measures" to restore the authority of Lagos in the Eastern Region, but soon full-scale civil war broke out. Finally, in January 1970 Biafran resistance collapsed, and the FMG reasserted its authority over the area. An estimated 1 to 3 million Nigerians died from hostilities, disease, and starvation during the civil war, and more than 3 million Igbo became refugees. The economy of the region was shattered. In several years, however, the state government achieved the rehabilitation of 70 percent of the industry incapacitated during the war. The federal government granted funds to cover the state's operating expenses for an interim period, and much of the war damage was repaired.

**Coups and Mostly Military Government:** In the postwar period, all significant political power remained concentrated in the FMG. The influence of Yakubu (Jack) Gowon, who had come to power in a 1966 coup, depended on his position as chairman of the Supreme Military Council, which was created in March 1967. The regime ruled by decree. In October 1970, Gowon announced his intention of staying in power until 1976, the target year for completion of the military's political program and return to an elected civilian government. But many Nigerians feared that the military planned to retain power indefinitely. In 1972 Gowon partially lifted the ban on political activity that had been in force since 1966 in order to permit a discussion of a new constitution that would pave the way for civilian rule. However, the debate that followed was ideologically charged, and Gowon abruptly terminated the discussion.

The Gowon regime came under fire because of widespread and obvious corruption at every level of national life. Inefficiencies compounded the effects of corruption. Crime also posed a threat to national security and had a seriously negative impact on efforts to bring about economic development. The political atmosphere deteriorated to the point where Gowon was deposed in a bloodless military coup in July 1975. The armed forces chose as Gowon's successor Brigadier (later General) Murtala Ramat Muhammad, a Muslim northerner. Muhammad was assassinated during an unsuccessful coup in February 1976, but in a short time his policies had won him broad popular support, and his decisiveness elevated him to the status of national hero. He had sought to restore public confidence in the federal government, reduce government expenditures on public works, and encourage the expansion of the private sector. He also set in motion the stalled machinery of devolution to civilian rule by a commitment to hand over power to a democratically elected government by October 1979.

Lieutenant General Olusegun Obasanjo, a Yoruba, succeeded Muhammad. Keeping the established chain of command in place, Obasanjo pledged to continue the program for the restoration of civilian government in 1979 and to carry forward the reform program to improve the quality of public service. In 1979, under Obasanjo's leadership, Nigeria adopted a constitution based on the Constitution of the United States that provided for a separation of powers among the executive, legislative, and judicial branches. The country was now ready for local elections, to be followed by national elections that would return Nigeria to civilian rule. Obasanjo also initiated plans to move the federal capital from Lagos to a more central location in the interior at Abuja. Ultimately, Abuja became the country's capital in December 1991.

**The Second Republic, 1979–83:** In 1979 five revamped parties competed in national elections, marking the beginning of the Second Republic. The presidential succession from Obasanjo to a civilian, President Alhaji Shehu Shagari, was the first peaceful transfer of power since independence. Nigeria's Second Republic was born amid great expectations. Oil prices were high, and revenues were on the increase. It appeared that unlimited development was possible. Unfortunately, the euphoria was short-lived. A number of weaknesses beset the Second Republic. First, the coalition that dominated federal politics was not strong, and in effect the victorious National Party of Nigeria (NPN) led by Shagari governed as a minority. Second, there was a lack of cooperation between the NPN-dominated federal government and the 12 states controlled by opposition parties. Third, and perhaps most importantly, the oil boom ended in mid-1981, precisely when expectations of continuous growth and prosperity were at a height. The ensuing recession put severe strains on the Second Republic.

**Return to Military Rule:** On December 31, 1983, the military seized power once again, primarily because there was virtually no confidence in the civilian regime. Allegations of fraud associated with Shagari's re-election in 1983 served as a pretext for the takeover, although the military was in fact closely associated with the ousted government. Ominously, the economy was in chaos. The true cost of the failure to use earlier revenues and foreign reserves to good effect now became apparent. The leader of the coup d'état was Major General Muhammadu Buhari, a Hausa whose background and political loyalties tied him closely to the Muslim north and the deposed government. The military regime tried to achieve two goals. First, it attempted to secure public support by reducing the level of corruption; second, it demonstrated its commitment to austerity by trimming the federal budget. In a further effort to mobilize the country, Buhari launched a "War Against Indiscipline" in the spring of 1984. This national campaign, which lasted 15 months, preached the work ethic, emphasized patriotism, decried corruption, and promoted environmental sanitation. However, the campaign achieved few of its aims.

The economic crisis, the campaign against corruption, and civilian criticism of the military undermined Buhari's position, and in August 1985 a group of officers under Major General Ibrahim Babangida removed Buhari from power. The Babangida regime had a rocky start. A countercoup in December 1985 failed but made it clear that not everyone in the military sided with the Armed Forces Ruling Council, which succeeded the Supreme Military Council. The most serious opposition centered in the labor movement and on university campuses. There was also considerable controversy over Nigeria's entry into the Organization of the Islamic Conference, an international body of Muslim states, in 1986. Buhari's regime had initiated the application, which Babangida allowed to stand. The strong reaction among many Christians proved to be an embarrassment to the regime.

Babangida addressed the worsening recession through the structural adjustment program of 1986. However, despite US$4.2 billion of support from the World Bank and the rescheduling of foreign debt, the recession led to a series of currency devaluations, a decline in real income, and rising unemployment during the second half of the 1980s. Babangida remained in power until 1993, when he ushered in an Interim National Government under the leadership of Chief Ernest Shonekan. This step followed the military's annulment of election results in June 1993.

In November 1993, General Sani Abacha seized control from the caretaker government and served as military dictator until his death in 1998. During his rule, Abacha suppressed dissent and failed to follow through with a promised transition to civilian government. In 1995, as a result of various human rights violations, the European Union, which already had imposed sanctions in 1993, suspended development aid, and Nigeria was temporarily expelled from the Commonwealth. Corruption also flourished, and Abacha was later found to have siphoned off oil revenues into personal bank accounts in Switzerland. In 2005 Nigeria began to recover US$458 million of illicit funds deposited in Swiss banks during the Abacha regime.

**Transition to Civilian Government:** Upon Abacha's death in June 1998, his chief of defense staff, Major General Abdulsalami Abubakar, assumed control and began to release political prisoners, including the former leader Obasanjo. Local government elections were held in December 1998, state legislative elections followed in January 1999, and federal legislative and presidential elections completed the transition to civilian government in February 1999. Obasanjo was elected president, and his party, the People's Democratic Party (PDP), won a majority of the seats in both the Senate and House of Representatives, amidst ever-present allegations of election irregularities. Fifteen years of military rule had come to an end, and Nigeria entered the longest period of civilian rule since independence.

Obasanjo succeeded in establishing civilian rule based on a multiparty democracy and launched a campaign against corruption, but despite a surge in oil revenues that buoyed the federal coffers, his administration faced a number of serious challenges. In 2000 religious tensions spiked following the imposition of sharia, or Islamic law, in 12 northern, predominantly Muslim states. These tensions hindered cooperation between the president and the National Assembly, among the states, and between the states and the federal government. In 2004 religious strife forced the government to declare a state of emergency in centrally located Plateau State. Ethnic strife further complicated matters, notably in the southeastern state of Benue, where tribal warfare broke out in 2001, and in the oil-rich Niger Delta, where the Ijaw tribe continues to conduct an insurgency against international energy facilities and workers.

Following his re-election in 2003, speculation had mounted that Obasanjo might seek a constitutional change that would permit him to run for a third term in 2007. However, in May 2006 the Nigerian Senate rejected a constitutional amendment that would have permitted a third term. Umaru Musa Yar'Adua, of the PDP, won the presidential election held in April 2007 and succeeded Obasanjo.

## GEOGRAPHY

**Click to Enlarge Image**

**Location:** Nigeria is located in West Africa on the Gulf of Guinea between Benin and Cameroon.

**Size:** Nigeria has an area of 923,768 square kilometers, including about 13,000 square kilometers of water.

**Land Boundaries:** Nigeria shares borders with Cameroon (1,690 kilometers) in the east, Chad (87 kilometers) in the northeast, Niger (1,497 kilometers) in the north, and Benin (773 kilometers) in the west.

**Disputed Territory:** Nigeria and Cameroon have held bilateral meetings to resolve disputes concerning the two countries' shared land and maritime boundary. In August 2006, Nigeria finally fulfilled its pledge to cede the Bakasi Peninsula, which juts into the Gulf of Guinea, to Cameroon, thus complying with the International Court of Justice's 2002 ruling in favor of Cameroon.

**Length of Coastline:** Nigeria's coastline along the Gulf of Guinea totals 853 kilometers.

**Maritime Claims:** Nigeria claims a territorial sea of 12 nautical miles, an exclusive economic zone of 200 nautical miles, and a continental shelf to a depth of 200 meters or to the depth of exploitation.

**Topography:** Nigeria has five major geographic regions: a low coastal zone along the Gulf of Guinea; hills and low plateaus north of the coastal zone; the Niger–Benue river valley; a broad stepped plateau stretching to the northern border with elevations exceeding 1,200 meters; and a mountainous zone along the eastern border, which includes the country's highest point, Chappal Waddi (2,419 meters).

**Principal Rivers:** Nigeria has two principal river systems: the Niger–Benue and the Chad. The Niger River, the largest in West Africa, flows 4,000 kilometers from Guinea through Mali, Niger, Benin, and Nigeria before emptying into the Gulf of Guinea. The Benue, the Niger's largest tributary, flows 1,400 kilometers from Cameroon into Nigeria, where it empties into the Niger River. The country's other river system involves various rivers that merge into the Yobe River, which then flows along the border with Niger and empties into Lake Chad.

**Climate:** Nigeria's climate is arid in the north, tropical in the center, and equatorial in the south. Variations are governed by the interaction of moist southwest monsoon and dry northeast winds. Mean maximum temperatures are 30° C–32° C in the south and 33° C–35° C in the north. High humidity is characteristic from February to November in the south and from June to September in the north. Low humidity coincides with the dry season. Annual rainfall decreases northward; rainfall ranges from about 2,000 millimeters in the coastal zone (averaging more than 3,550 millimeters in the Niger Delta) to 500–750 millimeters in the north.

**Natural Resources:** Nigeria's primary natural resources consist of natural gas, petroleum, tin, iron ore, coal, limestone, niobium, lead, and zinc. Nigeria has proven oil reserves of 36.2 billion barrels, the tenth largest reserves in the world. Proven natural gas reserves are estimated at 182 trillion cubic feet, the seventh largest reserves in the world and the largest in Africa. Estimates for oil and natural gas reserves are as of January 2007. The country also has an abundance of arable land.

**Land Use:** In 2005 Nigeria's land use was as follows: arable land, 33 percent; permanent crops, 3 percent; and other, 64 percent.

**Environmental Factors:** Urbanization and industrialization have led to a waste management crisis, resulting in widespread air, water, and soil pollution. Oil spills, natural gas flaring, automobile emissions, the open burning and dumping of waste, and improperly constructed landfills all contribute to serious environmental damage. Nigeria plans to phase out natural gas flaring by 2008 by converting natural gas into liquefied natural gas. Another major environmental issue is deforestation and the attendant loss of arable land as a result of logging, burning, and overgrazing by livestock. The area occupied by forests has been cut roughly in half since 1990.

**Time Zone:** Nigeria observes Nigeria Standard Time, which is Greenwich Mean Time plus one hour.


## SOCIETY

**Population:** As of mid-2008, Nigeria's population was estimated at 138 million, and the annual population growth rate was about 2.38 percent. Provisional results of the 2006 census indicate a total population of 140 million. Like its predecessors, this census has been controversial, given Nigeria's ethnic and religious rivalries, in particular the divide between the Muslim north and Christian south. Many observers, and southerners in particular, do not accept census results indicating that the north is more populous than the south. The significance of census data for political power and resource allocation exacerbates the controversy. When the last census was held in 1991, Nigeria's population was only 88.5 million according to official results, but many observers, including the World Bank, projected a total population of at least 120 million.

Nigeria's overall population density in 2006 was about 139 people per square kilometer. Much of the population is concentrated along the coast and in the north around Kano. Although Nigeria is slightly below average for the level of urbanization (about 45 percent), it nevertheless has one of the world's highest urbanization rates: an estimated 5.3 percent per year. The estimated net migration rate in 2008 was 0.25 migrants per 1,000 people.

**Demography:** In 2008 Nigeria's age distribution was estimated as follows: 0–14 years, 42.2 percent; 15–64 years, 54.7 percent; and 65 years and older, 3.1 percent. The birthrate was 39.98 births and the death rate, 16.41 deaths per 1,000 people. The infant mortality rate was 93.93 deaths per 1,000 live births. Life expectancy was about 47.8 years on average, or 47.2 years for males and 48.5 years for females. The fertility rate was 5.41 children per woman. The sex ratio at birth was 1.03 males per female.

**Ethnic Groups:** Nigeria has more than 250 ethnic groups. The most significant groups are Hausa and Fulani (29 percent), Yoruba (21 percent), Igbo (also seen as Ibo, 18 percent), and Ijaw (10 percent). Hausa and Fulani have traditionally dominated in the north, Yoruba in the southwest, Igbo in the east, and Ijaw in the Niger Delta. Rivalries among ethnic groups are a source of instability. Since 1991, questions about religion and ethnicity have not been included in the national census.

**Languages:** The official language is English. Other widely used languages are Edo, Efik, Fulani, Adamawa Fulfulde, Hausa, Idoma, Igbo (Ibo), Central Kanuri, Yoniba, and Yoruba.

**Religion:** Nigeria's population is split primarily between Islam (50 percent) and Christianity (40 percent). Muslims constitute the majority in the north and Christians the majority in the south. The remaining 10 percent of the population adheres to indigenous beliefs such as animism. In early 2006, following news of the publication of derogatory caricatures of the Prophet Muhammad in a Danish newspaper, anti-Christian riots broke out in Nigeria, and anti-Muslim reprisals followed. Churches and mosques were destroyed, numerous people were injured, and more than 100 were killed during the violence.

**Education and Literacy:** In 2004 Nigeria's adult literacy rate was 69.1 percent on average, with a higher rate for men (78.2 percent) than for women (60.1 percent). Nigeria provides free, government-supported education, but attendance is not compulsory at any level, and certain groups, such as nomads and the handicapped, are underserved. The education system consists of six years of primary school, three years of junior secondary school, three years of senior secondary school, and four years of university education leading to a bachelor's degree. In 2005 59 percent of girls and 68 percent of boys were enrolled in primary school. However, only 23 percent of girls and 28 percent of boys were enrolled in secondary school. In 2004 the Nigerian National Planning Commission described the country's education system as "dysfunctional." Reasons for this characterization included decaying institutions and ill-prepared graduates.

**Health:** The poor condition of health and health care in Nigeria is one of the factors responsible for an average life expectancy of only 47 years. Poor overall living conditions are another factor. In 2002 only 72 percent of urban residents and 49 percent of rural residents had access to safe drinking water. Only 48 percent of urban residents and 30 percent of rural residents had access to adequate sanitation. Many Nigerians devote one to three hours of their day to the chore of collecting water for domestic use.

In addition, the incidence of human immunodeficiency virus/acquired immune deficiency syndrome (HIV/AIDS) is very elevated. As of the end of 2005, about 2.9 million Nigerian adults were infected with HIV/AIDS, representing a prevalence rate of 3.9 percent. During 2005, about 220,000 Nigerians died from HIV/AIDS. Polio, tuberculosis (TB), and malaria also pose challenges. In 2007 the World Bank found that Nigeria had the thirteenth highest TB infection rate in the world and the fifth highest in Africa. In 2003 polio immunization efforts suffered a setback when the Muslim state of Kano halted vaccinations out of unsubstantiated fears of a Western conspiracy to sterilize the Muslim world and spread HIV/AIDS. Perhaps as a result, in 2004 some 792 Nigerian children were paralyzed by polio, up from 355 cases in 2003. In 2004 Nigeria accounted for 63 percent of polio cases worldwide. No improvement was registered in 2005, when polio cases rose to 801. Malaria remains a serious problem, with 2.6 million cases and 5,343 related deaths in 2003.

**Welfare:** From July 1994 until June 2004, private-sector employers and their workers were required to contribute to the Nigeria Social Insurance Trust Fund, which supported a defined benefit pension. The total contribution was 10 percent of an individual's wages: 6.5 percent from the employer and 3.5 percent from the employee. A separate pay-as-you-go plan, which suffered from poor administration, inadequate funding, and fraud, covered public-sector employees. Beginning on June 25, 2004, a new social insurance system based on the defined contribution approach replaced the prior arrangements in accordance with the Pension Reform Act of 2004. Under the new system, which is managed by the National Pension Commission, members of the military contribute 2.5 percent of their wages, and the military contributes 12.5 percent on their behalf, while public- and private-sector workers and their employers each contribute 7.5 percent.

## ECONOMY

**Overview:** Nigeria's economy is struggling to leverage the country's vast wealth in fossil fuels in order to displace the crushing poverty that affects about 57 percent of its population. Economists refer to the coexistence of vast natural resources wealth and extreme personal poverty in developing countries like Nigeria as the "paradox of plenty" or the "curse of oil." Nigeria's exports of oil and natural gas—at a time of peak prices—have enabled the country to post merchandise trade and current account surpluses in recent years. Reportedly, 80 percent of Nigeria's energy revenues flow to the government, 16 percent cover operational costs, and the remaining 4 percent go to investors. However, the World Bank has estimated that, as a result of corruption, 80 percent of energy revenues benefit only 1 percent of the population. Following a milestone agreement with the Paris Club of lending nations in 2005 and a similar agreement with the London Club of lending nations in 2006, Nigeria succeeded in eliminating almost all of its external debt. The agreements consisted of a combination of debt forgiveness and repayment from the country's energy revenues. Outside of the energy sector, Nigeria's economy is highly inefficient. Moreover, human capital is underdeveloped—Nigeria ranked 158 out of 177 countries in the United Nations Development Index in 2005—and non-energy-related infrastructure is inadequate.

During 2003–7 Nigeria attempted to implement an economic reform program called the National Economic Empowerment Development Strategy (NEEDS). The purpose of NEEDS was to raise the country's standard of living through a variety of reforms, including macroeconomic stability, deregulation, liberalization, privatization, transparency, and accountability. NEEDS sought to address basic deficiencies, such as the lack of freshwater for household use and irrigation, unreliable power supplies, decaying infrastructure, impediments to private enterprise, and corruption. The government hoped that NEEDS would create 7 million new jobs, diversify the economy, boost non-energy exports, increase industrial capacity utilization, and improve agricultural productivity. A related initiative on the state level is the State Economic Empowerment Development Strategy (SEEDS).

A longer-term economic development program is the United Nations (UN)–sponsored National Millennium Goals for Nigeria. Under the program, which covers the years from 2000 to 2015, Nigeria is committed to achieving a wide range of ambitious objectives involving poverty reduction, education, gender equality, health, the environment, and international development cooperation. In an update released in 2004, the UN found that Nigeria was making progress toward achieving several goals but was falling short on others. Specifically, Nigeria had advanced efforts to provide universal primary education, protect the environment, and develop a global development partnership. However, the country lagged behind on the goals of eliminating extreme poverty and hunger, reducing child and maternal mortality, and combating diseases such as human immunodeficiency virus/acquired immune deficiency syndrome (HIV/AIDS) and malaria.

After taking office in May 2007, President Umaru Musa Yar'adua embraced a policy known as Vision 2020 to transform Nigeria into one of the world's top-20 economies by 2020. Vision 2020 envisaged the enactment of a "Seven Point Agenda," consisting of the following points: power and energy infrastructure; food security and agriculture; wealth creation and employment; mass transportation; land reform; security (including bringing stability to the Niger Delta); and education.

A prerequisite for achieving many of these worthwhile objectives is curtailing endemic corruption, which stymies development and taints Nigeria's business environment. Former President Olusegun Obansanjo's campaign against corruption, which included the arrest of officials accused of misdeeds and the recovery of stolen funds, won praise from the World Bank. In September 2005, Nigeria, with the assistance of the World Bank, began to recover US$458 million of illicit funds that had been deposited in Swiss banks by the late military dictator Sani Abacha, who ruled Nigeria from 1993 to 1998. However, broad-based progress has been elusive and has not yet become evident in international surveys of corruption. In fact, Nigeria ranked 147 out of 179 countries in Transparency International's 2007 Corruption Perceptions Index and placed 108 out of 178 countries in the World Bank's 2008 Ease of Doing Business Index. Corruption mostly harms Nigerians themselves, but the country is widely known around the world for a fraudulent activity known as the "419" scam, which seeks to extort money from foreign recipients of letters and emails with the promise to transfer a nonexistent windfall sum of money.

**Gross Domestic Product (GDP):** In 2007 Nigeria had an estimated gross domestic product (GDP) of US$166.8 billion according to the official exchange rate and US$292.7 billion according to purchasing power parity (PPP). GDP rose by 6.4 percent in real terms over the previous year. GDP per capita was about US$1,200 using the official exchange rate and US$2,000 using the PPP method. About 60 percent of the population lives on less than US$1 per day. In 2007 the GDP was composed of the following sectors: agriculture, 17.6 percent; industry, 53.1 percent; and services, 29.3 percent.

**Government Budget:** In 2007 Nigeria's central government had expenditures of US$21.8 billion and revenues of US$20.5 billion, resulting in a budget deficit of about 6 percent. Nigerian tax authorities face the challenge of widespread tax evasion, which is motivated by complaints about corruption and the poor quality of services.

**Inflation:** In 2007 Nigeria's inflation rate was an estimated 6.5 percent, much lower than the double-digit rate in 2005. This sharp reduction represents progress toward one of Nigeria's goals under the National Economic Empowerment Development Strategy (NEEDS) program.

**Agriculture, Forestry, and Fishing:** The agriculture, forestry, and fishing sector constitutes about 17.6 percent of gross domestic product but employs up to 70 percent of the workforce. Agricultural products include cassava (tapioca), cocoa, corn, millet, palm oil, peanuts, rice, rubber, sorghum, and yams. Livestock products include cattle, chickens, goats, pigs, and sheep. In 2005 the total fishing catch was 579.5 metric tons. In the forestry subsector, roundwood removals totaled slightly more than 70 million cubic meters; no recent statistics are available for sawnwood production. The agricultural sector suffers from extremely low productivity, reflecting reliance on antiquated methods. Although overall agricultural production rose by 28 percent during the 1990s, per capita output rose by only 8.5 percent during the same decade. Agriculture has failed to keep pace with Nigeria's rapid population growth, so that the country, which once exported food, now relies on imports to sustain itself.

**Mining and Minerals:** Nigeria has abundant deposits of solid minerals, including barites, coal, columbite, gemstones, gold, graphite, gypsum, kaolin, marble, iron ore, salt, soda, sulfur, tantalite, tin, and uranium. Nevertheless, the mining industry, which exported significant amounts of coal and tin until the 1960s, has declined as publicly controlled infrastructure has deteriorated and the petroleum industry has grown in importance. Today mining accounts for only 1 percent of gross domestic product and is a minor employer. Mining suffers from extremely low productivity and high production costs. Nigeria is seeking to reinvigorate its mining industry through privatization and deregulation.

**Industry and Manufacturing:** Industry accounts for 53.1 percent of Nigeria's gross domestic product (GDP), much of which is attributable to the lucrative energy sector, and it employs about 10 percent of the labor force. The oil and gas sector accounts for 95 to 99 percent of Nigeria's export revenues. Manufacturing's share of export revenues is estimated at 1 percent. By contrast, in 2005 manufactured goods constituted the largest category of imports. In 2006 the capacity utilization rate of industry stood at 53.3 percent, a relatively low rate that policy makers hoped to increase by reversing capital flight and removing impediments to private-sector activity.

**Energy:** A member of the Organization of the Petroleum Exporting Countries (OPEC), Nigeria has proven oil reserves of 36.2 billion barrels, the tenth largest reserves in the world. Most of the reserves are located in the Niger River Delta. In 2006 Nigeria produced 2.4 million barrels per day (bpd) of oil, approximately 2.1 million bpd of which were exported. Nigeria ranks as the world's eighth largest exporter of oil and the United States' fifth largest source of imported oil. Nigeria hopes to increase production over the next five years but faces pressure from OPEC not to exceed its quota, which is set at 2.3 million bpd. In February 2006, the steady flow of Nigerian oil exports was hampered by attacks against oil facilities and kidnappings of oil workers staged by militants upset with the distribution of oil profits within Nigerian society. In fact, damage to one of Royal Dutch Shell's export terminals led to a 25 percent reduction in Nigeria's oil exports. This reduction has continued into 2008, as violence has worsened and many foreign oil workers have left the country. In January 2008, the Ijaw Youth Council, a group representing the Ijaw ethnic group, announced that it was supporting the militants. Such continued violence could pose another impediment—in addition to OPEC's concerns—to Nigeria's plans to boost production.

Proven natural gas reserves are estimated at 182 trillion cubic feet, the seventh largest reserves in the world and the largest in Africa. In 2005 Nigeria produced 791 billion cubic feet (bcf) of natural gas, 425 bcf of which were exported.

Recoverable coal reserves amount to 209 million short tons (mmst). In 2004 Nigeria produced only 0.02 mmst, all of which was consumed domestically. Nigeria's coal industry suffers from extremely low productivity and high transportation costs.

Only 40 percent of Nigeria's population has access to electricity, although the government plans to expand access to 85 percent of the population by 2010 through a rural electrification program. In 2005 Nigeria produced 23 billion kilowatt-hours of electricity, exceeding domestic consumption of 17 billion kilowatt-hours. Nigeria's electric network operates well below its capacity of 5,900 megawatts, and power outages are commonplace. Foreign electric power companies have been encouraged to build independent power plants to help meet the demand for electricity.

**Services:** Services accounted for an estimated 29.3 percent of gross domestic product and employed roughly one in five workers in 2006. The most important branch of the services sector is banking and finance.

**Banking and Finance:** In 2006 Nigeria's banking sector successfully completed a consolidation program under the supervision of the Central Bank of Nigeria, which has regulatory authority over the entire financial sector. From a total of 89 banks, many of them marginal, 25 relatively well capitalized deposit banks have emerged. Even before the consolidation, loan assets and deposit liabilities were highly concentrated. In addition to deposit banks, Nigeria has hundreds of community banks and a small number of specialized development and mortgage banks. A similar consolidation is planned for the insurance sector. In 2007 Nigerian banks such as Intercontinental Bank and Guaranty Trust were the beneficiaries of significant foreign investment. Contrary to modern practice, many financial transactions in Nigeria are conducted in cash rather than with bank letters of credit.

**Tourism:** In 2005 Nigeria received more than 2.7 million tourists. The largest contingents came from Niger (620,658), Benin (393,215), Liberia (107,401), and Cameroon (107,108). In 2004 tourism receipts totaled US$49 million. The Nigerian government encourages its citizens to visit tourism destinations within the country through various financial incentives. Concerns exist regarding the quality of amenities and personal safety.

**Labor:** In 2007 Nigeria had an estimated labor force of 50.1 million. Unemployment was estimated at 4.9 percent in 2007. In 2006 the unemployment rate was 5.8 percent overall; urban unemployment of 12.3 percent exceeded rural unemployment of 7.4 percent. According to the latest available information from 1999, labor force employment by sector was as follows: 70 percent in agriculture, 20 percent in services, and 10 percent in industry. Labor unions, which have undergone periods of militancy and quiescence, reemerged as a force in 1998 when they regained independence from the government. Since 1999 the Nigerian Labor Congress (NLC), a union umbrella organization, has called numerous general strikes to protest domestic fuel price increases. However, in March 2005 the government introduced legislation ending the NLC's monopoly over union organizing. In December 2005, the NLC was lobbying for an increase in the minimum wage for federal workers. The existing minimum wage, which was introduced six years earlier but has not been adjusted since, has been whittled away by inflation.

**Foreign Economic Relations:** Nigeria's foreign economic relations revolve around its role in supplying the world economy with oil and natural gas, even as the country seeks to diversify its exports, harmonize tariffs in line with a potential customs union sought by the Economic Community of West African States (ECOWAS), and encourage inflows of foreign portfolio and direct investment. In October 2005, Nigeria implemented the ECOWAS Common External Tariff, which reduced the number of tariff bands. Prior to this revision, tariffs constituted Nigeria's second largest source of revenue after oil exports. In 2005 Nigeria achieved a major breakthrough when it reached an agreement with the Paris Club to eliminate its bilateral debt through a combination of write-downs and buybacks. In 2006 Nigeria reached a similar agreement with the London Club of lending nations. Nigeria joined the Organization of the Petroleum Exporting Countries in July 1971 and the World Trade Organization in January 1995.

**Imports:** In 2007 Nigeria imported about US$39 billion of goods. In 2006 the leading sources of imports were China (10.7 percent), the United States (8.4 percent), the Netherlands (6.2 percent), the United Kingdom (5.8 percent), France (5.6 percent), Brazil (5.1 percent), and Germany (4.5 percent). Principal imports were manufactured goods, machinery and transport equipment, chemicals, and food and live animals.

**Exports:** In 2007 Nigeria exported about US$62 billion of goods. In 2006 the leading destinations for exports were the United States (48.9 percent), Spain (8 percent), Brazil (7.3 percent), and France (4.2 percent). Oil accounted for 95 to 99 percent of merchandise exports, and cocoa and rubber accounted for the remainder.

**Trade Balance:** In 2007 Nigeria posted a US$23 billion trade surplus.

**Balance of Payments:** In 2007 Nigeria achieved a positive current account balance of US$14.6 billion.

**External Debt:** In recent years, Nigeria has made tremendous progress toward the elimination of its national debt, which stood at US$37.5 billion in 2005. That year Nigeria and a group of international creditors known as the Paris Club agreed to eliminate the country's bilateral debt. Under the agreement, the Paris Club cancelled US$18 billion of bilateral debt, and Nigeria paid back the remaining US$12.4 billion. In 2006 Nigeria followed up with a similar agreement with the London Club group of creditors, leading to the elimination of US$2.15 billion of related debt. The remaining external debt, estimated to be in a *de minimis* range in 2008, is not expected to be prepaid, but should be serviced in a timely manner.

**Foreign Investment:** In 2006 Nigeria received a net inflow of US$5.4 billion of foreign direct investment (FDI), much of which came from the United States. FDI constituted 74.8 percent of gross fixed capital formation, reflecting low levels of domestic investment. Most FDI is directed toward the energy sector. Between 2008 and 2020, Nigeria hopes to attract US$600 billion of FDI to finance its Vision 2020 policy to transform the country's economy into one of the world's 20 largest.

**Foreign Aid:** As of August 2007, World Bank assistance to Nigeria involved 23 active projects with a total commitment value of about US$2.67 billion. Since Nigeria joined the World Bank in 1961, the World Bank has assisted it on 123 projects. In October 2005, the International Monetary Fund (IMF) approved a two-year "policy support instrument" designed to promote the growth of the non-oil sector and to reduce poverty. In a review of the program in March 2008, the IMF noted progress in Nigeria's macroeconomic performance, average non-oil sector growth of 8.5 percent, and a reduction in inflation to about 6 percent. However, despite an improvement in the economic situation of the majority of households, poverty remained high.

**Currency and Exchange Rate:** The Nigerian currency is the naira (NGN). As of mid-July 2008, the exchange rate was about US$1=NGN117.

**Fiscal Year:** Calendar year.


## TRANSPORTATION AND TELECOMMUNICATIONS

**Overview:** Decaying infrastructure is one of the deficiencies that Nigeria's Vision 2020 policy seeks to address. The government has begun to repair the country's poorly maintained road network. Because Nigeria's railroads are in a parlous condition, the government is trying to rectify the situation by privatizing the Nigerian Railroad Corporation. Similarly, the government is pursuing a strategy of partial port privatization by granting concessions to private port operators so that they can improve the quality of port facilities and operations. Nigeria's airports and civil aviation system have a poor reputation for efficiency and safety, and government-owned Nigerian Airways is struggling. In the telecommunications sector, mobile telephones are more widely disseminated than landline phones, and Internet use revolves mainly around cybercafés.

**Roads:** Nigeria has roughly 113,000 kilometers of surfaced roads, but they are poorly maintained and are even cited as a cause for the country's high rate of traffic fatalities. However, in 2004 Nigeria's Federal Roads Maintenance Agency (FERMA) began to patch the 32,000-kilometer federal roads network, and in 2005 FERMA initiated a more substantial rehabilitation. Since its inception, FERMA has repaired about 100 major roads out of about 500 targeted by the agency. The emphasis has been on repairs rather than maintenance because the poor condition of the roads does not justify maintenance at this point.

**Railroads:** As of 2006, Nigeria's poorly maintained rail system consisted of 3,505 kilometers of narrow-gauge track. The country has two major rail lines: one connects Lagos on the Bight of Benin and Nguru in the northern state of Yobe; the other connects Port Harcourt in the Niger Delta and Maiduguri in the northeastern state of Borno. Nigeria is enlisting China's support to expand its rail network. In November 2006, the China Civil Engineering and Construction Corporation signed an US$8.3 billion contract to build a new standard-gauge rail link between Lagos and Kano in the north. A second rail link is contemplated between Port Harcourt and Jos in the interior. Altogether, a 20-year strategic plan calls for the construction of 8,000 kilometers of standard rail lines.

**Ports:** The Nigerian Port Authority (NPA) is responsible for managing Nigeria's ports, which have fallen behind international standards in terms of the quality of facilities and operational efficiency. Recognizing that the government lacks the funding and expertise to modernize facilities and to run the ports efficiently, the NPA is pursuing partial port privatization by means of granting concessions to private port operators. Under the terms of concession agreements, the government has begun to transfer operating rights to private companies for 10–25 years without relinquishing ownership of the port land. Nigeria's principal container port is Lagos Port, which consists of separate facilities at Apapa and Tin Can Island and has a rail connection to points inland. Lagos Port, which has a container handling capacity of 22,000 twenty-foot equivalent units (TEUs), handles two-thirds of Nigeria's non-oil trade. The main petroleum outlets are Delta Port Complex, including Burutu, and Port Harcourt, a transshipment port located 66 kilometers from the Gulf of Guinea along the Bonny River in the Niger Delta. Relatively modern and efficient onshore and offshore terminals managed by multinational oil companies handle most oil and gas exports.

**Inland Waterways:** Nigeria has 8,600 kilometers of inland waterways. The most important are the Niger River and its tributary, the Benue River.

**Civil Aviation and Airports:** Nigeria has 18 international and regional airports. The principal airports are Murtala Muhammad Airport in Lagos and Mallam Aminu International in the northern state of Kano. Three other international airports are located in Abuja, Kaduna, and Port Harcourt. Overall, Nigeria's airports, whether international or regional, suffer from a poor reputation for operational efficiency and safety, but the government has launched an inspection and rehabilitation program. Private domestic air carriers have won business at the expense of Nigerian Airways, whose assets were liquidated by the government in 2003 in response to rampant corruption.

**Pipelines:** In 2007 Nigeria had 4,347 kilometers of pipelines for oil, 3,949 kilometers for refined products, 3,071 kilometers for natural gas, 156 kilometers for liquid petroleum gas, and 124 kilometers for condensates. Various pipeline projects are planned to expand the domestic distribution of natural gas and to export natural gas to Benin, Ghana, Togo, and, potentially, even to Algeria (where a Mediterranean export terminal is located). Energy pipelines are subject to sabotage by militant groups or siphoning by thieves.

**Telecommunications:** Television and radio broadcast stations currently operational in Nigeria include 83 AM, 36 FM, and 11 shortwave radio stations and three television stations. Recent information on the number of radios and televisions is not available. In 2006 Nigeria had about 8 million Internet users, many of whom relied on equipment at cybercafés. In 2007 Internet hosts totaled 1,968. In 2006 more than 32.3 million mobile cellular telephones and 1.7 million main lines were in use.

## GOVERNMENT AND POLITICS

**Political System:** Nigeria is a federal republic with a presidential system. The constitution provides for a separation of powers among the three branches of government. General elections held in February 1999 marked the end of 15 years of military rule and the beginning of civilian rule based on a multiparty democracy. General elections were held for the third consecutive time in April 2007. The victor was Umaru Musa Yar'adua, who assumed the presidency on May 29, 2007. In May 2006, the Nigerian Senate rejected a constitutional amendment that would have permitted President Olusegun Obasanjo to run for a third term.

**Constitution:** Nigeria's current constitution, the fourth since independence, went into effect on May 29, 1999. Modeled after the U.S. Constitution, it provides for a separation of powers among a strong executive, an elected legislature, and an independent judiciary. Critics of the constitution complain that the federal government retains too much power at the expense of the states. Although the constitution proclaims personal freedom and a secular state, it also permits Muslims to follow sharia, or Islamic law.

**Branches of Government:** Executive power is vested in the president, who is simultaneously chief of state and head of government. The president is eligible for two four-year terms. The president's Federal Executive Council, or cabinet, includes representatives from all 36 states. The National Assembly, consisting of a 109-member Senate and a 360-member House of Representatives, constitutes the country's legislative branch. Three senators represent each of Nigeria's 36 states, and one additional senator represents the capital city of Abuja. Seats in the House of Representatives are allocated according to population. Therefore, the number of House members from each state differs. Members of the National Assembly are elected to a maximum of two four-year terms. The judicial branch comprises the Supreme Court, the Court of Appeal, the Federal High Court, and, at the state level, high courts, sharia courts, and customary courts. The president appoints members of the Supreme Court subject to confirmation by the Senate.

**Administrative Divisions:** Nigeria is divided administratively into the Federal Capital Territory (Abuja) and 36 states, which are organized into the following six zones: South–West Zone— Lagos, Ekiti, Ogun, Ondo, Oshun, and Oyo; South–South Zone—Akwa, Bayelsa, Cross River, Delta, Edo, Ibom, and Rivers; South–East Zone—Abia, Anambra, Ebonyi, Enugu, and Imo; North–West Zone—Kaduna, Kano, Katsina, Jigawa, Kebbi, Sokoto, and Zamfara; North–Central

Zone—Benue, Kogi, Kwara, Nassarawa, Niger, and Plateau; and North–East Zone—Adamawa, Bauchi, Bornue, Gomber, Taraba, and Yobe.

**Provincial and Local Government:** Each of Nigeria's 36 states has an elected governor and a House of Assembly. The governor is elected to a maximum of two four-year terms. The number of delegates to the House of Assembly is based on population (three to four times the number of delegates each state sends to the federal House of Representatives) and therefore varies from state to state within the range of 24 to 40. Nigeria's states are subdivided into 774 local government areas, each of which is governed by a council that is responsible for supplying basic needs. The local government councils, which are regarded as the third tier of government below the federal and state levels, receive monthly subsidies from a national "federation account." Critics contend that the division of the country into so many districts is a vestige of military rule that is arbitrary, wasteful, and inefficient.

**Judicial and Legal System:** Nigeria's legal system is based on a combination of statutory (legislative) law, English common law, customary law, and, in the north, Islamic law (sharia). Nigeria's federal and state courts apply statutory and English common law, whereas local courts recognize the legitimacy of customary and Islamic law. Bribes paid to influence judges and delays in bringing cases to trial sometimes impair the fair and efficient administration of justice. These deficiencies partially explain the popularity of Islamic law in the 12 northern states. Nevertheless, sharia is criticized for the imposition of draconian penalties, although no death penalties have been carried out in recent years. Testimony from women and non-Muslims also carries less weight in Islamic courts.

**Electoral System:** The president and members of the bicameral National Assembly, consisting of a 109-member Senate and a 360-member House of Representatives, are elected to a maximum of two four-year terms. Universal suffrage at age 18 applies to all elections. Winning candidates are determined according to the British first-past-the-post system, whereby a plurality of the votes ensures victory. Also under this system, members of the National Assembly represent distinct geographic constituencies. International observers and several Nigerian parties alleged fraud, irregularities, and politically motivated violence in the most recent elections in 2007. Former U.S. Secretary of State Madeleine Albright, who observed the elections, called the electoral process "a step backward."

**Politics and Political Parties:** Presidential and legislative elections were last held on April 21, 2007. President Umaru Musa Yar'adua was elected to a four-year term for the first time. The runner-up was former military ruler Muhammadu Buhari, who represented the All Nigeria People's Party (ANPP). Yar'adua's party, the People's Democratic Party (PDP), also won a majority of the votes in the elections for the Senate (53.7 percent) and House of Representatives (54.4 percent). The most successful opposition party in the legislative elections was the ANPP. Also participating were the All Progressives Grand Alliance (APGA), the Alliance for Democracy (AD), the National Democratic Party (NDP), the People's Redemption Party (PRP), and the United Nigeria People's Party (UNPP).

**Mass Media:** The government controls and regulates most of Nigeria's broadcast media through the National Broadcasting Commission. Radio is the most important mass medium for reaching general audiences because it is inexpensive and does not require literacy. The federal government owns stations affiliated with the Federal Radio Corporation of Nigeria, individual states control other stations, and still others are privately owned. The Voice of Nigeria broadcasts in Arabic, English, French, and five indigenous languages. Some Voice of Nigeria broadcasts are aimed at domestic audiences; others, primarily shortwave, are transmitted around the globe. Similar to the market for radio broadcasts, the federal government owns two stations affiliated with the National Television Authority, various states have their own stations, and private operators broadcast by satellite. Nigerians also obtain news via Voice of America, the British Broadcasting Company (BBC), and Deutsche Welle. In contrast to the broadcast media, the print media are dominated by private publications, a situation that is more amenable to criticism of the government. Nigeria has 14 major daily newspapers, but only one—the *New Nigerian*—is government-owned. The country also has six newsweeklies and various tabloids. The government does not restrict access to the Internet, which is most widely available at cybercafés.

**Foreign Relations:** Traditionally, Nigeria's foreign policy has revolved primarily around African affairs and emphasizes political and economic cooperation, peaceful dispute resolution, and global nonalignment. However, under the new Yar'adua administration, Nigeria has shifted its foreign policy focus toward economic relations, including attracting US$600 billion of foreign direct investment by 2020. Regionally, Nigeria pursues tariff harmonization and the long-term goal of a customs union via the Economic Community of West African States, which it was instrumental in founding. Nigeria is also active in the New Partnership for Africa's Development, which seeks to improve economic conditions in Africa by eliminating trade barriers to exports and attracting investment and development aid. In August 2006, after lengthy negotiations, Nigeria relinquished its claim to the disputed Bakasi Peninsula, finally complying with the 2002 decision of the International Court of Justice in favor of Cameroon over control of the disputed territory. Since mid-1998, Nigeria's relations with the United States have improved steadily in accordance with Nigeria's transition from military rule to democracy. Nigeria has also supported the U.S.-led war on terrorism. In March 2006, Nigeria's then-president, Olusegun Obasanjo, met with President George W. Bush in Washington, DC, to discuss the U.S.-Nigerian relationship. With a touch of drama immediately before the meeting, Nigeria turned over the exiled former Liberian leader Charles Taylor to a United Nations (UN) court in Sierra Leone to face allegations of war crimes. Nigeria is seeking a permanent seat on the UN Security Council.

**Membership in International Organizations:** Nigeria belongs to the following international organizations: African, Caribbean, and Pacific Group of States; African Development Bank; African Union; Commonwealth; Economic Community of West African States; Food and Agriculture Organization; Group of 15; Group of 24; Group of 77; International Atomic Energy Agency; International Bank for Reconstruction and Development (World Bank); International Chamber of Commerce; International Civil Aviation Organization; International Confederation of Free Trade Unions; International Criminal Court; International Criminal Police Organization; International Development Association; International Finance Corporation; International Fund for Agricultural Development; International Hydrographic Organization; International Labor Organization; International Olympic Committee; International Maritime Organization; International Monetary Fund; International Organization for Migration; International Organization for Standardization; International Red Cross and Red Crescent Movement; International Telecommunication Union; Multilateral Investment Geographic Agency;

Nonaligned Movement; Organisation for the Prohibition of Chemical Weapons; Organization of the Islamic Conference; Organization of the Petroleum Exporting Countries; Permanent Court of Arbitration; United Nations; Universal Postal Union; World Customs Organization; World Federation of Trade Unions; World Health Organization; World Intellectual Property Organization; World Meteorological Organization; World Tourism Organization; and World Trade Organization.

**Major International Treaties:** Nigeria is a party to the following nonproliferation agreements: Biological Weapons Convention, Chemical Weapons Convention, Nuclear Non-proliferation Treaty, and Partial Test Ban Treaty. Regarding the environment, Nigeria is a party to international agreements on Biodiversity, Climate Change, Desertification, Endangered Species, Hazardous Wastes, Kyoto Protocol, Law of the Sea, Marine Dumping, Marine Life Conservation, Ozone Layer Protection, and Wetlands. Shortly after September 11, 2001, Nigeria ratified a Mutual Legal Assistance Treaty with the United States. The treaty, whose ratification had been held up for 12 years, includes provisions for cooperation on anticrime, antidrug, and counterterrorism initiatives.


## NATIONAL SECURITY

**Armed Forces Overview:** The military, which ruled Nigeria for all but four years during the period 1966–99, is now subject to civilian rule. Internal divisions, public support for democratic rule, and the armed forces' poor image are all factors militating against a coup in the current environment. Nigeria's military, by far the largest in sub-Saharan Africa, is primarily used in international peacekeeping operations.

**Foreign Military Relations:** Nigeria's military has participated in several peacekeeping operations in sub-Saharan Africa to help raise the country's profile as a regional power. Nigeria remains committed to this policy despite the death of two Nigerian soldiers assigned to the African Union's peacekeeping mission in Darfur, Sudan, in October 2005. The United States and China are vying for military influence in Nigeria. In February 2006, Nigeria's vice president criticized the United States for not protecting Nigeria's oil industry from attacks by insurgents affiliated with the Movement for the Emancipation of the Niger Delta (MEND). Although the U.S. government had provided military technical assistance and training, it had not followed through completely with the promised delivery of high-speed patrol boats, apparently out of concern that the Nigerian military was involved in the sale of stolen oil to criminal gangs. As a result, Nigeria was turning to China to supply patrol boats. China has been ramping up its military presence in the oil-rich Niger Delta to safeguard its own energy-related investments. In December 2007, Nigerian President Umaru Musa Yar'adua met with U.S. President George W. Bush to discuss U.S. plans to set up a joint military command for Africa, one of whose missions would be to provide counterterrorism support in the Gulf of Guinea. Although initial press reports indicated that Yar'adua had endorsed the plan, he later clarified that he had requested U.S. support for an African version of the command and had not offered the U.S. basing rights in Nigeria.

**External Threat:** Nigeria's neighbors do not pose an external threat. Foreign support for Islamist militant groups in the north and cross-border criminal activities may be the most acute external threats.

**Defense Budget:** In 2006 Nigeria's military budget was about US$768 million, representing less than 1 percent of gross domestic product.

**Major Military Units:** Nigeria's armed forces consist of 85,000 active-duty personnel assigned as follows to the various services: army, 67,000; navy, 8,000; and air force 10,000. The army is organized into one armored division, one composite division (motorized, amphibious, and airborne), two mechanized divisions, and one Presidential Guard brigade. The navy's headquarters is at Lagos, the western command is at Apapa (near Lagos), and the eastern command is at Calabar (inland along the Cross River, near the Bakasi Peninsula). In 2000 the air force moved its headquarters from Lagos to Abuja.

**Major Military Equipment:** The army has 270 main battle tanks (although 100 Soviet-era T–55 tanks may not be serviceable), 150 light tanks, 342 reconnaissance vehicles, more than 427 armored personnel carriers, 431 towed artillery, 27 self-propelled artillery, 25 multiple rocket launchers, more than 330 mortars, and unspecified numbers of antitank guided weapons, recoilless launchers, air defense guns, surface-to-air missiles, and surveillance vehicles. The navy has two principal surface combatants, 20 patrol and coastal combatants, two mine warfare vessels, one amphibious vessel, and five support and miscellaneous vessels, but not all of these ships may be ready for action. Navy aviation has four helicopters of doubtful serviceability. The air force has 84 combat aircraft and five attack helicopters.

**Military Service:** The age requirement for voluntary military service is 18 years.

**Paramilitary Forces:** Nigeria's paramilitary forces, including the port security police and the Ministry of Internal Affairs' security and civil defense corps, are estimated at 82,000 personnel.

**Foreign Military Forces:** On December 8, 2005, the United States and Nigeria reached an agreement to patrol the Niger Delta jointly to prevent insurgent attacks on energy installations. However, implementation of the agreement has been delayed, and the Nigerians have turned for security assistance to China, which, like the United States, is heavily invested in Nigeria's energy industry.

**Military Forces Abroad:** Nigeria has participated in United Nations (UN) operations and missions in Burundi, Democratic Republic of the Congo, Ethiopia and Eritrea, Ivory Coast, Liberia, Sierra Leone, Sudan, and Western Sahara. In September 2005, Nigeria withdrew 120 police officers serving in the UN Congo mission because of accusations that they had engaged in sexual abuses.

**Police:** The Nigeria Police Force, which was established in 1930 and most recently reorganized along more decentralized lines in 1988, now ranks as the largest police force in Africa, with 371,800 officers as of June 2007. The president appoints the inspector general of police, who is responsible for the operational control of the force. As the ultimate police authority, the president may issue directives to the inspector general regarding the maintenance of public order. The police face the challenge of combating trans-border gang activity, human trafficking, and a wide variety of financial crimes, particularly the so-called 419 scam, whereby criminals persuade targets to advance them money in order to receive a larger payment. The police have extensive powers, including the power to arrest without a warrant, conduct searches and seize property, and detain suspects. According to a March 2008 report by the U.S. Department of State, abuses by the Nigerian police, including the use of lethal force against suspects, are commonplace. In July 2005, Human Rights Watch issued a highly critical report on police torture and deaths in custody in Nigeria. The report found that attempts to reform the police had been largely symbolic and failed to address torture adequately. In November 2007, Human Rights Watch called for an independent investigation into reports that the police had shot and killed more than 8,000 Nigerians since 2000.

**Internal Threat:** The two principal threats to domestic security are violence in the Niger Delta and sectarian strife between Muslims and Christians. The catalyst for violence in the Niger Delta, where the country's energy sector is concentrated, is the indigenous population's dissatisfaction with their impoverished condition, despite the wealth generated by the area's resources, and the environmental degradation caused by energy-related development. This disenchantment has spawned a militant group known as the Movement for the Emancipation of the Niger Delta (MEND). MEND is seeking a more equitable distribution of Nigeria's oil wealth so that it benefits the local population, particularly the indigenous Ijaw tribe. Since early 2006, MEND militias have attacked oil installations and kidnapped foreign oil industry workers in an effort to press their demands. These actions have led to a sustained 20 percent reduction in Nigeria's oil production. In April 2008, MEND damaged pipelines belonging to Shell and Chevron as part of its violent campaign—known as Project Cyclone—to cripple Nigeria's oil export industry. In September 2007, Ijaw militia leader Henry Okah was arrested in Angola, and in February 2008 Angola turned him over to Nigerian authorities. In May 2008, a Nigerian court ordered Okah to stand trial for arms dealing and treason behind closed doors. The trial is expected to spur further violence. However, it was also reported in May 2008 that the Nigerian government is pursuing a deal with the Ijaw Youth Council, a group affiliated with MEND, to have the militias end their attacks in exchange for cash.

In addition to MEND, another internal security threat is sectarian violence, which has cost the lives of more than 10,000 Nigerians since 1999. In the north, where Muslims predominate, Islamic groups have introduced sharia, or Islamic law, in 12 states, causing many Christians to flee. Similarly, in the south, where Christians predominate, Muslims complain about discrimination and treatment as second-class citizens. In early 2006, reports about derogatory cartoon depictions of the Prophet Muhammad in Danish newspapers led to a fresh outbreak of sectarian violence; more than 100 people were killed, and numerous churches and mosques were destroyed. According to a May 2005 report from the United States Commission on International Religious Freedom, Islamic extremist activities in the north are being funded by foreign sources. Although the report did not specify the foreign sources, it cited Libya, Saudi Arabia, and Sudan as funding the construction of mosques and religious schools and asserted that Nigerian clerics trained in Saudi Arabia had been indoctrinated to promote hatred and violence against non-Muslims. The Nigerian government is particularly concerned about an Islamist group known as "Hisbah" that enforces sharia in the northern state of Kano. In February 2006, the government alleged that Kano was training 100 militants belonging to this group in intelligence gathering and jihadist operations at the behest of foreign powers.

**Terrorism:** The U.S. Department of State has commended Nigeria for "forging an anti-terrorism consensus" in sub-Saharan Africa following al Qaeda's attacks against the United States on September 11, 2001. In fact, Nigeria has coordinated the U.S.-led Trans-Sahara Counterterrorism Initiative, which conducts counterterrorism exercises in the region to prevent extremist groups from taking root. The Movement for the Emancipation of the Niger Delta (MEND), which seeks to drive out foreign energy companies and force the government to share energy-derived wealth with its citizens, disclaims any affiliation with any external terrorist group such as al Qaeda. Nevertheless, it engages in acts of violence, including sabotage of energy-related infrastructure and the kidnapping of foreign oil workers. As of April 2008, the U.S. Department of State did not include MEND on its official list of foreign terrorist organizations, so it might be more appropriate to characterize MEND as an insurgency.

**Human Rights:** In its 2007 report on human rights practices around the world, the U.S. Department of State found that Nigeria's human rights record was "poor." According to the report, Nigerian government officials and police were responsible for "serious abuses," including politically motivated killings; the use of lethal force against suspected criminals and hostage-seizing militants in the Niger Delta; beatings and even torture of suspects, detainees, and convicts; and extortion of civilians. Other abuses included violence, discrimination, and genital mutilation directed against women, child labor and prostitution, and human trafficking. Compounding these abuses was the application of Islamic law (sharia) in 12 northern states. Sentences imposed under sharia included amputations, stonings, and canings, but no death sentences were carried out. In addition, the Department of State noted restrictions on the freedoms of speech, press, assembly, religion, movement, and privacy.